Teaching the Wind Plurals

D1493512

Also published by Robson Books

Fluffy Dice
The Dust Behind the Door

Teaching the Wind Plurals

NIGEL FORDE

Robson Books

First published in Great Britain in 1991 by Robson Books Ltd,
Bolsover House, 5–6 Clipstone Street, London W1P 7EB

British Library Cataloguing in Publication Data
Forde, Nigel
    Teaching the wind plurals.
    I. Title
    821.914

    ISBN 0 86051 718 7

Typeset by Bookworm Typesetting, Manchester
Printed in Great Britain by
Billing & Sons Ltd., Worcester

for Hilary

Contents

A Moment of Pure Love in the Festival Hall   11

Walking the Dog   12

Processional   14

Between Two Years   15

A New Song   17

Interferences   19

Demoralizations   20

Lessons in Deportment   22

After Elgar on the Malverns   23

Spring Song in Winter   24

Die Tageszeiten   25

Telling Stories   26

Bogey Man   28

Water Ways   30

Hack's Field, November   32

Home for the Elderly   34

Party Piece   36

Still to Come   37

Estuary   38

The Audition   39

Wolf   40

On the Beach: Logos   41

Regina v. Gallus   42

Home Thoughts   43

Siciliana   44

Child's Play	46
Nine Lessons in Painting a Nativity	47
Edmund Loves Cordelia – True	49
Cold Song	51
Quintet for a New Year	52
The Edge of the Wood	56
Conventional Signs	57
And Some of the Larger Pieces That You See Are Called Uncles	58
Child With a Red Spade	60
Waterscapes	61
Rebecca Dancing	63
Four Elegies	65
Cloudburst	68
Bee in the Window	70
August	72
Same Again	73
Methods of Winter	74
The Hard Harvest	75
Mirror in an Empty Room	76
Rain on Hazel Leaves	78

Acknowledgements

are due to the editors of the following newspapers and journals in which several of these poems first appeared: the *Observer*, *Country Life*, the *London Magazine*, the *Countryman*. Three were published in the Arvon Foundation Anthology, 1985 and many were broadcast on the Radio 4 series Mixed MetaFordes.

I owe a particular debt to David Thomas and Gillian Clarke for their tireless encouragement and for their help in preparing this collection; and I have been the beneficiary of great friendship and wisdom from John Moat and John Fairfax.

N.F.

A Moment of Pure Love
in the Festival Hall

You sing an A softly, not knowing that you do it.
The orchestra make scribbles in the air
looking for theirs, in amber, black and gold
and find the one you knew. You tap your chin
with a slow fist and do not look at me.

Will you meet Dido, sepulchres and lilies?
Midnights or vineyards, or the lapping down
of indoor silences like hyacinths?
Stern, pertinent simultaneous equations,
elegies, dreams or memories' dead estates
unfallowed by this rainfall in the air?

I am a pile of selves, and one is yours,
one mine, one music's, but the ghost of yours
as you are music's ghost when you're not here.
I leave my silence to its own devices
and follow random movements of your hair,
content to see you far in unawareness,
content, at last, to hear and not to hear
cellos speaking long, plum-coloured vowels
and woodwind turning shadows in your eyes.

Walking the Dog

She invents angles at full tilt.
She is Einstein to my Euclid
with ears that say 'Eureka'.
Today, again, we look at the world
for the first time.

I am breezy but slow;
stirring a twig, a stalk.
I watch her gusting; trying
to surround herself.
A black and white wind,
a force eight dog.

The sun, leaf-shaped through branches,
licks her again and again
but cannot taste her at that speed.

Paths run out and stand around
awkwardly, trying to look
like bracken or bramble. She
never runs out, not even of paths,

but she cranks up a crane on his
seven-league legs; teaches the blackbird
semaphore, the robin morse code,
and explodes starlings like bombs.

Her shadow, faultlessly, keeps up.
Only when she poses for Landseer on a rock,
exhaling whole landscapes,
inhaling fresh data,
does it hang from her, useless.

When dusk falls she flickers beside me,
another quiet sliver of it.
I push open the door
and she lets me in.

Her rum-and-butter eyes tilt
as I move towards bed.
I turn at the door;
her tail thumps once, proposing a theorem.

Processional

at York Minster

Saints, roses, in their holy jigsaws
move down like water in the moving sun;
stone which space, or space which stone ignores,
finds and translates to equilibrium

a possession of silence, adroit harmonies
turning like motes, a noiseless dust of prayer;
an ancient tongue alive with courtesies
spoken to the smart, vernacular air.

Light of light born kindling the rose
and stiff-winged angels drawn in frost of stone;
glass, music, sculptured martyrdoms dispose
safe, distant deaths. A long flower of sun

climbs up through countless histories; dissolves,
petal by petal, where the darkness falls.

Between Two Years

This morning the window opens
like a slow squeeze of leather;
the hinges double-glazed
with ice.

Batsqueaks next;
a glass newspaper dissolving.

From behind the curtain
I can see how the world looks
when I can't see how the world looks.

Convex.

After the silent thud
of the icicle
that drops
a surprised mouth into the snowdrift,
the hills hiss with the sound
of taped silence.
They have been going on all night.

The earth is a fiction
invented by these elegant
tons of weightlessness;

solid deceptions, white lies of declivity
shouted into no one's ear.
The sky believes them,
the ceiling repeats them.

Snow is a candle all day,
it is the word 'moon' in translation,
it is innuendo;
a bark of silence.

I slot myself into the tall drive
with a spade. My boots make
four creaks at a time,
and then the snow says
DUNLOP

I say to myself 'snow snow snow
snow snow' until
it is the wrong word for snow,

and hear, quite close,
the first real sound of the day
when water
slips through its own fingers
and away.

A New Song

for Patrick

As abstract as you are singular,
the candid world you've made
tries all ways of accepting you;
finds smiles best.
You breed them easily in
your silences that tiptoe round the room,
your small flesh an endearment
now made man.

You scorn the search for form,
significance, by being both
and in the centre, where
admirable occurrences of springtime
stop to stare at your slow swing
on the edge of sleep,
your careful catalogues
of all you will not keep.

We lay aside troubles; never cease
to smile at what you may become
(another homeward smile in summer rain,
a brown angle of sun at the sea's lips,
a watcher of candles, a small, awkward squad
on school-days) or what you are now:
unworded but faultless in the pure
language of paradigm;

King of the beasts – the wall-eyed lamb,
sad elephant and all the idiot rabbits
that trample your cot. King-like, too,
you bestow new titles such as 'Mother',
'Father', on those you love; dub cousins
in your wisdom, elevate aunts.
Click! The generations shift; you have
space, now, in which to tread.

Soon we will people your familiar
walks with ogres, princes, dragons,
millers' sons and magic words
folded in magic quinces. Now the air
around you conjugates angels, gladness.
You do not know, but you've begun;
surrounded by inconceivable ideas
of which you're one.

Interferences

The owls follows his echo round a tree
and into darkness, rustling like a spill
of wind. His ghost is snagged inside my head;
alien, foreigner, mouthorganing in
on private wavelengths. Sliding past a cloud,
the moon rolls round with vile and fragile grin
and clamps his windowed white across my bed.

Half as dark again, the garden holds
moonlight prisoner, locked with owl and wind.
Half shiver is for silence, half for cold;
but inside are the normal walls. The mind
withdraws to light and safety, and the blind
owl, wind, silence, under the house's lid
darkly repeat where repetition's hid.

Demoralizations

1

Once upon a time there was a tortoise;
he is the sympathetic character.
There was also a hare, far from villainous
but not much liked, you understand,
being a good judge of his own considerable
capabilities and a bit of a failure
as far as tolerance was concerned.
He, vainglorious, confident, a little sad,
challenged the good but bewildered tortoise
to a race. Tortoise humbly accepted;
many eyebrows were raised, sighs sighed.
The day of the race dawned – believe it
or not – bright and clear. At the word
'Go' the hare sprang with his mad Marchness
into a speck and trampolined the dizzy
horizon. Tortoise coughed gently and moved
a foot or two forward. Yes, the outcome
seemed obvious and, indeed, before
tortoise had shaved a shadow's length
from his purposed plod, hare was back,
panting, all teeth and windy fur
and the race over.

Moral: Don't imagine you'll ever know
how the world is going to go
even if you've read Aesop.

2

A certain man was journeying
from Jerusalem to Jericho
when he fell among thieves.
They stripped him and beat him and departed
leaving him for dead. Now by chance
there came a certain priest that way,
and when he saw the man, naked,
bleeding and helpless, he rushed
across from the other side of the road,
bandaged him and anointed him
with healing balsams, dressed him
in fine raiment, put money in his purse
and took him to his own home
until he was recovered.

Moral: It is better to do some good
than merely to point a moral.

3

On a high branch, shaded with leaves
and green as a wave of the sea,
hung a bunch of sour grapes.
A fox with a long thirst and short legs
tried for a whole sunstruck day
to reach them, with snapping jaws
and body flung again and again
into the twisting wind. As he left
the tree he reassured himself
that the grapes were probably sour.

Moral: You don't have to be
successful to be right.

Lessons in Deportment

Oh, my good girl, my wise girl,
just when everything was tidy!

Just when Newton had taught the earth
how to behave with gravity;
just when Einstein had introduced it
to its relatives; when Gödel had educated it,
statisticians had counted it,
philosophers had framed it and visiting professors
from American universities had presented it
with honorary degrees, diplomas
and several certificates of merit,
you came and stood on it.

Oh, my bad girl, my silly girl,
just when everything was tidy.

Perhaps we will say nothing
and hope the clever people will fail to notice
that when I pass your window, apples
leap from grass to branch,
coal shoots into bud, I love
therefore I am; and Newton,
Einstein, Gödel, turn in their graves.

After Elgar on the Malverns

for Tod

Alone among apostles I am unmoved; finding
no necessary sequence which will join
landscape to inspiration. But I see

smoke from below crawl sideways (nobilmente),
and a dog (presto) in a ditch – all later markings,
as is the thin con moto of the cars.

No enigmas in this air; no Falstaff
on a folding picnic-stool. Only the damp
woods at late morning. And that's Bax.

Somewhere a bird fails to be a grass-stalk;
knocks two lumps of air together and stares
upwards at the echo. But that's Bartok.

And a skylark, if it is a skylark, has the cheek
to drop whole bars of Ralph Vaughan
Williams from invisible ledger lines.

In the throat of the kingdom-drinking wind
I listen for the fruitful speech of angels,
and hear only my meek and modern ostinato;

yet on these reverberate hills American ladies
(Dorabellas, Nimrods) bend, and do not fail
to gather green crotchets and wild semibreves.

Spring Song in Winter

for H.D.E.F.

Lost for words, and far from them; a chime
of twigs; cow-sweet murmurs from the farm,
and long years falling, month by month. Time
bites less rawly now. Less sharply come

the unguarded hungers. Green calligraphies
each spring, from ash and beech he loved, will keep
ancestral watch with flowers at their knees
and echo his unexaggerated sleep.

A glimmering owl slides down loops of night,
articulate of strangeness as of pain,
dissolving both to harmless archetype.

So, gratefully, we change, yet stay the same,
as old hills gather sheaves of summer light;
as birds reassemble after rain.

Die Tageszeiten

Telemann's sunrise has been beaten
by the real thing. Two wasps
at a pear's mouth dance a slow pavane.
I am early for rehearsal, have time
to stoop and kiss the oldest Dolmetsch
of them all, who leads her ghosts
around the garden blinking with butterflies.

The lawn's a green zebra of damp tree-shadow,
stippled with semiquavers from the music room
following her like geese. Too old
for viol or recorder now, her freckled
fingers play the buttons on her blouse:
a frail, true descant repeating, da capo,
all the music that her youth had made.

'If you've time,' she said, 'I'll tell you about Ezra:
Ezra Pound – what a wan, wild man; I met him
with my husband, Arnold. He took a liking
to both the lute and . . . Look, they're going in
to start the Telemann. Off you go, now.
I mustn't interrupt the music.' So I went,
and found the garden empty when we'd done.

Four days later. I am early again for
'Die Tageszeiten'. Mabel's in her chair
collecting the sun in her blue lap.
'. . . and to the clavichord which, as you know,
Arnold had re-invented.' She went on
and finished the story. And on went the sunlight
translating seeds to red geraniums.

Telling Stories

It was what you would expect:
the Prince got her in the end.

Not by a fugitive and cloistered virtue;
it took seven armies and a lot

of justifiable wrath, patience,
humility and personal sacrifice,

But he did it; while you listened,
sofa-safe, moated by firelight,

smiling to hide your yawns.
We've been through so much together:

chapters of accidents, nights
bump-full of things, desperate

voyages, dark kingdoms and O
What Big Teeth Granny Dear.

Tonight, however, I look out
expecting in our garden to see

real Gerda searching for real Kay,
or a caravan through York's Arabian night;

a frog that looks just a little
different. A third son just about to do

just the right thing. And I wonder,
as I watch your bottom wag upstairs

out of the firelight into the dark,
what wolf in Granny's clothing,

what cold frog in what nocturnal forest
waits with open, archetypal arms.

Bogey Man

Something to do with The War, they said:
we would not understand. The warnings,
and there were many, were horridly
understated: 'Best not to . . .',
or 'Pitiable' they said, 'but even so . . .'

                                           Pity
was strange to us; fear we understood
and piled ourselves beside the normal fire.
'Half-roasted for him!' said a daring one;
we laughed in safe, sociable chorus.

                                    But he was bad.
He was AntiChristmas; he was a poker into eyes
and a sackful of ugly lumps of coal.
He could do things to your teeth; he was
Straw-Peter's grandson; he knew Trolls;
he lived under the bridge, up to his bum
in green water; ate leeches, frog spawn, toads
as well as boys; had limbs like us
but bit on the Marsh Monster's language;
warts he had, and sometimes wore the grasshopper's
savage, metalled face.

The night wind
rustled him up from ditches, and
(accustomed to finding 'Rupert's friends
hidden in the picture') we saw
his unskinned head in every knuckle
of the nightwood. The copse crawled
with corpses and with him.
He frightened the daylight out of afternoons.

Coming from the farm one morning,
he loomed at me from nowhere. I stood,
brave as a bagpipe, shouting silent terror.

He waved his grossly un-misshapen arms:
'Lovely' - pointing to the sky, his lovely,
lonely eyes aswim – 'Oh, lovely,
lovely, lovely!'

Water Ways

I sit and watch water taking several
thousand years to erase a rock
from the world's history.
I have to leave before the end.

Its slappings and plaitings,
its wet ropes of mistranslated light
are an illusion created
by the accidental sharps and flats
of a rock. Catch it in a bucket
and it goes dead.

Left to itself it does tricks
you'd laugh at if it weren't water.
For example:

it sits on otters.
It joggles the moon to a jigsaw
and then solves it; wraps air up
in water and kicks it out. It
has a disarming way of laughing at itself
after dark. It even hides
behind glass – and it can!

In winter it is
something you can walk on
in a quite unholy way
and hardly notice the miracle.

I like water best
when it stands trees perfectly
upon their heads
and leaves them there.

Hack's Field, November

A rook in the sky – a black rag in a white one –
rubbed the untouched-by-hand of the mist
and then became it.

The mist shawled, unmoving, from invisible nostrils
twice as big as England, wherever that was.

It Tipp-Exed out the glaring misprint
of the sun and pencilled in twilight.

It turned torch beams solid,
cracking them against pantomime trees
as noiselessly as paint on wool.

It made generalizations about oak, holly, beech,
but didn't name names or go into detail.

It heaved hills over their own horizons
and left a veil of hawthorn hedge, a stile:
two entries in a glossary of distances.

It curtained the tiny theatre of the spider
where all matinées had been cancelled.

It spawned soft stars on my cheek
and on the bare rim
of the hogweed's broken cartwheel.

It steamed off Constable and found Turner.

Only the cows were unsurprised
by a sudden world of milk; tearing
with their rubber scythes at the roots of it
and patiently wiping the dirty windscreen of their bums.

Home for the Elderly

Somewhere a scent has gone cold. Each day
is a dislocation, a feat of memory

nudged by the wrong faces, opening
familiar doors into unfamiliar spaces.

A photograph album in a lap is
a battered phrasebook from a foreign land;

it lisps precarious, uncertain idioms:
'at home' for instance, 'Our Tibby' or 'Lottie's girl',

bewildering news from nowhere, delivered
between knitting and the loud pastels of TV

while disciplined flowers from nurseries tell
perfect lies about cottage gardens.

On the wall is one graceless print –
a birch, a lake, a pathway – tinted

like Turkish delight, trapped in plastic;
a non-existent place that says

there is, there was, never anything more
(beyond the swirls of turquoise carpet,

the serious furniture, the stern, sharp
centre light) than this encumbrance of now:

ordered absence, consolation by proxy
and, every dreadful day, the smiling women

with tea, books and white trolleys
bearing unbearable kindnesses.

Party Piece

Your voice sounds awkward in the silence
which turns the room to stare,
through a thickness of thin air
that coincidence is piecing
with the noise that is not there,
at the silence that is missing.

What of you was left, I wonder,
when the talking had to stop?
You could hear a conversation drop;
and I catch the look in your eyes
as the conscious chatter goes off
at a tangent of surprise.

A mote of stillness stays with us;
a point of balance when
the gone and going blend,
and as the clock moves forward,
with a secret look again,
we agree that words are awkward.

Still to Come

In his dry cellars he experiments
on the musculature of words;
on ligaments, on tendons,
on delicate fibre-analysis.

His glittering equipment is made
by the finest craftsmen.
His collection of specimens is legendary,
his labelling meticulous.

He formulates at perfect temperatures
perfect equations. Even his muse,
to be helpful,
has assumed a hunched back.
But nothing moves.

Whatever lightning he pulls down
from rhetorical storms, whatever current
snaps through his slabs,
the catalogued cadavers stare up
through sutures at his white ceiling.

One day he'll find it, though;
some accidental energy he can't control
and cold, hideous words
will stagger through the howling night
and terrorize whole villages, whole worlds.

Estuary

The avocet stands
    on his grass-stalk legs which,
      entering the water
don't enter the water, but bend
    back into an avocet
      water-tinted, rippling
on the slack of a tide
    where the sun
      has spilled paint
all day, and now
    plays lapidary on wood,
      or bone, or pebble
or the sea, which leaves
    behind a hundred hundred
      miniatures of estuary
and goes, again, to find
    whatever it was it left far out
    at the slow horizon
where the sun inches down
    through blue, pearl, silver
      resonances of dusk
to a slack water which begins
    everything twice
    and which
ripples, ripples
    with the shadows
      of avocets.

The Audition

She stoops towards the voices in the stalls;
defenceless, fledgeling in the working-lights.
Actressy-graceful, arms clasped under breasts;
in black skirt over leotard and tights.

Her tiny heartbeat flicks a pool of dark
on, off, on, off under her ribs. She'll do
the Shakespeare first: it's four sizes too big.
Her little voice makes truth ill-fitting too.

Just so she pauses, looks or turns upstage;
just so she shakes her waterfall of hair.
A technique; like the mediocre mime,
trapped in a trite, glass box that isn't there.

The words she's learned, but not their dangerous reasons,
reasons that words outlive our deaths to learn;
her hopes themselves might teach her suffering. Only
I wish her no suffering, while I watch her turn
a world of grief to trivial conceit
above her lovely legs and pert, poised feet.

Wolf

Wolf cleaves to himself,
is the bones of snow,
fits darkness like a glove.

Wolf is in for the kill,
out for himself,
does not admit to mistakes.

Wolf is seldom at a loss,
learns quickly,
is not above cheating.

Wolf fears only what he sees,
always dies tragically,
looks noble in pictures.

Wolf has relations: dog, fox;
does not recognize them.
Has more of man about him than we like.

On the Beach: Logos

You echo the smooth skin of rocks and sea
in curves of shoulder, willing nakedness;
a silhouette still secret in undress,
moon-flecked with blue like lichen on a tree.

Logos and sea between your spread thighs spread,
as you stand flinging syllables of stone
as if you'd lose all meaning but our own
new knowledge – or old, newly interpreted.

I lap you, smooth you and your warm flesh-grain,
while lightning fans the long Ionian sky;
breast, belly and that tiny beard where thigh
meets thigh and where we ache to meet again;

a midnight harvest of my body, grown
too safe in love, too fond of words unsaid,
safe now in you again. I turn a head
to where my cold, tall alphabets are thrown

lifetime by lifetime in the mythic sea.
Your soft prow falls on me and falls on me.

Regina v. Gallus

*In 1474 a cock was executed in Basel
for the crime of laying eggs.*

Counsel for the defence argued reasonably,
if briefly, for clemency owing to the defendant's
home background. Mother strangled by person
or persons unknown one Christmas Eve;
never knew his father; kept apart
from opposite sex during formative years;
ancestors, immigrants or transportees,
had history of pugilism.
And evidence was at best circumstantial
including one plastic egg, said to be
a plant by all the witnesses.

The judge, however, was concerned
about the effect on young people,
and there was still the arson case
involving two glow worms,
the thievish magpie, the transvestite poodle,
the claustrophobic crab and the fish
who walked by himself.

No, it was the electric perch, undoubtedly.
We can't be doing with basilisks
In a civilized society.

Home Thoughts

Standing at the edge of the wood
I take a moment to admire the house
which, like all familiar things,
hugs itself beneath the unfamiliar snow;
trying to look like a Christmas card –
succeeding, no doubt, to a stranger's eye.

The roof, for instance, soft as a moth
with moon and stars. The windows
glowing with log or candle flame.
It tucks itself neatly into what surrounds it;
has a protective air; is insulated
against the darkness; is, yes, beautiful.

For snow has made the eye accept
an architecture taste would never dare:
Gothic icicles rise to support a roof
scooped and Rococoed by Regencies of wind.
The porch has an Early Norman encrustation.
Overnight the garden has turned formal.

Of course you cannot see the broken bottles
that would scar a hand; the rusty
debris in the thorns – relic of what worked
once upon a time; the deadly nails
laid bare by decay. Snow is like that.
My footsteps are going to start a thaw.

Siciliana

for Vicky

The eyes poise first. Then the fingers.
Flute lifted, a mirror
for magisterial Bach, hungry
for his lean, black semiquavers.

She threads the siciliana
taut with responsibility.
She and Bach
both no longer mine.

She is older at each cadence
fearlessly inhabited
with slow, flautist's smile.

A cool skein of notes, eggshells;
a skin round a purr of breath
or the impossible sound
of grey becoming blue
as air translates, miraculously,
to air.

She narrates impossibilities
as clouds and water,
methods of sunlight
or mercury or speedwell;
in a world still full of beginnings
she breathes her tightrope
and dances on it.

Her body no trouble to her
and in her eyes
the formidable shapes of silence.

Child's Play

for Tamsin

I had trespassed.
                    'No! Not there!'
'What?'
            For a second I saw blood
on the carpet; something smashed;
tried to find patience enough to lose
at one fell swipe.
                    'That's the river!'
So, thankfully, I slipped on Dad's role:
'Sorry! I'm being silly – I'll
step over.'
                    'You'll have to jump.'
I started by the sideboard and cleared it
apparently, landing safely beside the sofa.

And I watched for a moment the foam
whorl and blister about her feet
as she stepped deliberately among
the shallows, with customary bear
and plastic teapot; absorbed, careful,

undaunted by radio or table-lamps
lining the banks. I marvelled at
her single-mindedness, just as, later,
her tucked in bed, I marvelled while
I spilled minnows, gudgeon, from her shoes.

Nine Lessons in Painting a Nativity

1
The painter first invents himself.

2
This panache of snow and straw, these
jutting stars are internal landscape.
Fill in the sky afterwards: it has been
reasonable, you might say, all day.

3
There is a discipline of edges,
rims; of delineations. The world
is, finally, artificial.
It speaks Latin.

4
Do not try to reproduce moonlight
as if it were a mother-tongue.
The moon has vast histories and revels in them.

5
Not there. Not in the middle:
that is where we shall put one of the kings.
Make his face recognizable.

6

The angels, as if with a single sense,
will tread white air on fantastic wings.
Even they must be disposed
according to the tactful principles
of composition.

7

The world is full of artificial things;
your work is the work of a comedian.
Belief, you see, knows always
what it believes is not true.
Believe.

8

An immaculate, folding sea,
the dark thorn. Good. Now
paint me a startle of silence: lean
at least towards truth.

9

Last of all the painter invents himself.

Edmund Loves Cordelia – True

The eyes of those who know are on Cordelia
though Lear has all the words. Just off stage left
Another Part of the Heath is placed, inch-perfect;
for everything's decided in advance,
rehearsed and set. What shall Cordelia speak?
What's in the script: such as 'I'm sure my love's
more ponderous . . .'; and Edmund, aside, tonight
will watch the play, not do the *Guardian* crossword
in the spill of light from the prompt desk. There she is:
honest madam . . .

             How can you tell? She said
'I think', not 'know' but 'think'.

                    A small
pistol shot is fired off in his stomach
as they approach the casting off, the curse –
O God, give her the curse; dear Nature, hear!
Into her womb convey sterility,
Dry up in her . . .

           The end of the scene. She passes
with a glance. So young and so untender?
How can you tell if already she's a third
more opulent than the rest?

              Backstage is dark;
conversation is impossible.
Her cigarettes are in the dressing-room;
she'll hear him on the tannoy. He can fall
back on technique. A glib, a mannered Edmund
is quite acceptable. She'll make him suffer;
it serves him right. Tonight, though, there's a new,
desperate detachment in the scene.
It gets applause.

         Is she or isn't she though?

One version has a happy ending: Edgar
(the one from RADA) gets Cordelia.
Never Edmund. Life confuses Art.
To hell with applause: is she or is she not?

The play's a footnote, life's the text. Each phrase
however innocent, holds landscapes of regret.
I serve you, madam. Come, unbutton here.
Did your letters pierce the Queen? Now, gods,
stand up . . .!
                    A scene change; interval in ten.

Ripeness is all. The empty green-room smells
of Leichner, coffee, of mortality.
Cornwall mooches through, flicks Gloster's eye
casually into the air and catches it.
Five weeks of rep and then back to the dole,
then pantomime in Bradford. She'll be off
to do a walk-on at the RSC,
unless . . .
                    Far down the flaking passageway
the girls' door opens. Look, her lips, look there.
She turns and stands as if she'd lost a kingdom.
What shall Edmund speak? Love, and be silent?
He's a handsome Bastard in his black.
                                        On cue
their eyes meet and the ASMs shake out
ounces of thunder from the darkened wings.

Cold Song

A badger grandfathers home
in his old pyjamas. Light thins
as one bird leads to another.

By a process of illumination
last night's woodcut becomes pastel.
Damp trees tilt at their shadows' end.

The sun picks out a hill and climbs inside it;
licks the almost white almost green.

Swaying from the byre, a warm cow
disappears behind its breath
with a brief, empty, seashell sound.

I am unskinned for this season
or any season. Poor, forked creature
I disappear behind the sounds I make.

Quintet for a New Year

This poem was commissioned by the Dean and Chapter of York Minster to commemorate the 500th anniversary of the ending of the Wars of the Roses. The union of the houses of York and Lancaster was made visible by the marriage of Henry VII and Elizabeth of York.

I

They are royal,
this is the difference. They come
not empty-handed or ignorant,
not wantonly, in jest;
nor will they be without pain
for this long forgiveness.

But they are royal and are royal reasons
for the crack of trumpets, the soft elision
of eleisons on stone,
the whisper of lawn or velvet
under a hand empty of the axe.

The cathedral, Adam of Michelangelo
stretched on the world's ceiling,
lifts a finger up to God and holes
the heavy grisaille of winter cloud,
rips mist, bends winds, stops birds,
who flick their shadows in its eye,
shakes bells into the mad, January sky,

fractures sunlight, noiselessly as snow,
and stands it in tall octaves, in long
afternoons of dusk.

II

The North Sea still bellows, shoulders
its cold, unpuncturable muscles
at the cliffs.

Air on the moorland shocks
with its bite of second steel;
and, while kings raise fine emblems
over tombs where faces of the dead
are decent, composed,
well-dressed in marble,
out here death is not well-documented,
is less formal.
Out here, the things that do not happen
have happened.

III

Silences swing to
behind the noise of birds,
of the obsessive, wasp-faced sheep.

The stars have names, are useful:
with the plough you could plough
or find your way home by it.

Cassiopeia, Perseus, Orion,
full of stories for the fireside.

Now he who ploughed or found his way
home to the bubbling, fire-gashed logs,
he who most was providence, is dead;
hacked and hidden under earth,
under the advancing, turreted corn,
the next year's broken bread;
the homely crop where love
and words for love were born.

IV

A different century brings only
a new, unbroken heart, warring
in its own way; cloistered,
cabinned, celled, it seems
to smile but through the lips of wounds;
obedient to the starched priest
in white linen, or the cold anthem,
to the censer's swing or the owl's call –
the unearthly vespers of the earth.

It spills nothing, overflows
with no forgiveness; guards itself
against a Pentecost. It puts
a safe ring in Creation's nose.

The tall windows lean to see
themselves in parody:
Christ smashed in fire of sun
upon the stones.

V

They are royal. This
is winter and the end of winter.

He looks for the first time
into her brave eyes,
and unused landscapes tilt
and stretch between them.

There he sees
only
the sun-bloom on gules and gold,
only
the darkness over parched farms.

The Edge of the Wood

Light replacing itself soundlessly
with light, could be water but is leaf,
shifting its shallows, making metaphors
in five fathoms of sun.

A thickness of brown air relating itself
to different distances, could be trout
but is thrush, out of his depth in tree,
gargling with spring air.

Quick squirrels flicker up and through
beech caves, reflecting, refracting.
One twig dribbles a spider. He floats
lagooned in leaf.

At the wood's edge I stand unsure
of flying fish or swimming bird
or shock of trees' surf, tide of sun,
but in my element.

Conventional Signs

The line of dots, here on the map,
is a way of saying 'footpath'.
The smouldering bull, when you get there,
is a way of rubbing them out.

The battleground (crossed swords)
is grave-grey tarmac; the church
with a tower is a tower
with no church; the well
(when you get there)
is choked, soppy with autumns.

When you get there,
the windmill (this sign here)
you'll find pure bone: the last sails spilled the air
and went to make a chicken-house,
a wagon, long ago.

The folly, when you get there,
is bruised and cracked
like a mason's fingernail.
It stirs the leaves
with the four winds it can no longer afford.

Forgive me (when you speak
that significant word 'love')
if I tremble at the desecrations
I will find, the legendary falsehood,
when we get there.

And Some of the Larger Pieces
That You See Are Called Uncles

for Fionn

A small, daily miracle; and you
are separate now.

Not separate enough to say
hallo to, but you've come
suddenly. You are.
As if to be were easy.

You lie in a loud tangle of birthdays.
Only one of them
your own.

Beside your cot is the world
we left there on the last night
before you were born. Now
it contains you. Elementary
metaphysics, and easy for
the finger of God, but some of us
like to be surprised by it still.

This is the world, then. It contains,
apart from you and me (and I
am one, according to Shelley,
of its unacknowledged legislators):

calves, that make far woodwind sounds
in brimming meadows; owls
that do the same thing after dark;
lupins, shoelaces, mineral deposits
and the Royal College of Heralds.
A variety of hats, sundials, people
who look a bit like someone else you know,

restored water-mills, presents
from Weston-super-Mare; hippopotamuses,
things with lids, lighthouses, gloves,
Reader's Digest Condensed Books,
things without lids, and one
Great Pyramid of Cheops.

Someone has also invented waves,
silk hayfields, music
and the considerate stars.
We're keeping them for you.

All of a sudden
I'm worried that you're not going
to like them.

There are things you can change.
Already your limbs stammer
as sharp as words. You've made
your first, tiny addendum
to the world's dictionary
as you take fistfuls of air
and squeeze them dry.

Child With a Red Spade

She slaps at the sea with a red spade.
It retreats with an affronted noise
like a friendly uncle.

It comes back
to nibble her into a scream
with a tickle of icy foam.
She chuckles the Sea-Tamer's chuckle
and does it again.

It's a good game. The seaweed
nods at its knitting; the mussels
in the gallery dribble from their
idiotic mouths; we can all
join in the chorus.

I watch her quick, fearless ankles
looped with glass, wet with sun,
bully the tide unmercifully.

And I see not her, but in its cold
black teeth, horribly astride
a rumbling mile of muscle,
such sad captains smacking
the flinted waves, crying
'Naughty sea!
Naughty, naughty sea!'

Waterscapes

1

A multi-coloured sea shuffles itself
and deals wave, wave, wave, wave
into the rib-cages of sand which store
such manifold continuities
and then finesse reflections, paradigms
of watercolour sky and cloud.

2

The thick rip of grass
sounds like the smell of the word 'breakfast'.
According to the lake
the deer walk on stilts, perfectly
rehearsed; their antlers tick
in the loud silence. They tread
on thin shadows that, at evening, lean
another way. One bird,
then two, then three.

3

Fathom, fathom:
the humdrum of the sea, endless
as separations are endless.
A slow, black tonnage
which, where it meets a beach
is ounces; eyelashes under a sky of peach.

4

The square, flake-white with heat;
from the fountain's rim, rags ripped
from water drop; and when they meet
water there's a slippery sound
that could be Greek. The big sun
sews a shilling on each pleat.

5

Verticals, bare, unbent, are incantation
or beatitude. Amen, says the grass,
this is the way of iron; this is the way.
The only liquid thing, a pool
uneasy in a spool of wind.

6

Before dawn an old man goes by
with a lantern. The farm sways,
sways like water; shuts its eye.

Rebecca Dancing

You unfold, oh, soft as snow,
a slow geometry like light
inside a shell.

You move without adverbs, your every noun
hull down on horizons of your own creation
where nothing is, but all's becoming.

I need help in this new universe
you've made; where hairsbreadth
of finger tilts
and all the weighty freight of physics
turns to miracle.

You move in the thought of colour.
Flecks of gold
spin from your shoulders
and greens lean into darkness
as you turn. I have seen you kick
vermilions from the air which you inhabit;
I have seen your special way with silver.

Then, hey adagio! Your body
vanishes into what it is: alliteration,
flesh made word;

into random eternities which poise
for a second every second. You unmake me,
like music.

I do the best I can,
hopeless, despairing surrealist,
I run outside into real space, real time,
and build you a sunman.

Four Elegies

for D.A.H.

i

Here are the suburbs of separation;
the featureless landscapes unmoored
from the mother-country.

The language is bland,
is pity's Esperanto and has
no history, no appetite.

There should be trees but there are none.
The cathedral spires are down;
the green close is concrete;
at every turn there is hard glass
in which we see our own faces.

The streets – this is the worst thing –
sometimes look familiar
out of the tail of the eye;
but they are blank, faceless
in long, modern afternoons
and comfortable dusk comes never. We walk
as in dreams, arriving nowhere
at the wrong speed.

You've left us
a world you never walked on.

No wonder that we stare
at the inscapes of your absence;
searching the dreadful map
of a new town. Over and over again
we find only that loud tautology,
the black, insistent arrow tipped with poison:
YOU ARE HERE.

ii

Accomplishments of daylight hold the trees
in falls and floors of mist, making their close
translations of these green celerities.

The moon narrates the world in terms of white;
so form is fact and sharpness more than shade,
another truthful method of the light.

The sound of trees is what they make of air
or squirrel's footfall, owl's metonymy
which was, which will be, but which is not there.

And so with you. Your lively truth is still
a narrative discovered in translation
which now is our vernacular, and will

be fabled bread and wine of all our words,
be graze of dawn, birds at their harpsichords.

iii

Easily you taught us what the hard words mean:
'husband', 'father'. We'll use those words again
in an after-winter season one day when
the brown wound in the churchyard's grown to green.

iv

Compton beach
paved
with sunset flicked away
through the rear window.

You drove us
homewards
through stone smells, through
embassies of stars.

The sting of the sea
stayed
to salt our talk. We clambered,
sun-lagged, through family jokes.

The bright hills
see-sawed;
everything the world did
was a comely thing to do;

and all about,
stubble
on the fallen fields
empty in the full moon.

Cloudburst

The air went with the spent light
down a swift, sick plughole in the sky;
and it was the rain.
The mad rain jamming the space lungs
grasped for. Sudden, barbarous,
savagely unurban.

Each suicidal shaft dug deep
into long dryness, smashed into stars
on pavements, varnished whole
half trees. Just like that.

Drains gargled with it, garbled it
and whaled it into streets.
Rooves spat it back, it roped
from gutters, clopped and bellied
in hollows it made or met. It stamped
the gardens silly and with grape-shot
raked the windows till they bled with it
and still it walloped down; it hissed,
clattered, drummed and thrummed steel-bands
in alleyways, skinned cats to sealions,
shipwrecked boxes, cans, sang songs
in bottles, whacked water with itself,
clapped its own exit as resoundingly
fell silence.

Then the tiny plash and dribble
from leaf and eaves. Hair-of-the-dog.

Small talk after the hellfire sermon
of the rain. Human, eloquent.

Bee in the Window

You'd think, by now, that evolution
would have given bees a sense of glass;
not so. This one, pang! he went;
little brown fist in glove, beating
the nothingness before him; scribbling
invisible graphs of puzzlement on
his easy element turned traitor.

His argument was sound, Euclidean: he knew
the shortest distance between two points –
the hairspring tongue and the flouncing
mallow filling all his eyes – but now
this hard space held him; his legs
trod madly all geometries and found
a new dimension not to dance through.

I watched his one action replay after
another, his relentless browbeating of the
more-than-meets-the-eye his eye had met;
his legs landlubbered, his bad buzz
clenching, unclenching. He dipped
out of my shadow; pang! again, as he
believed what he couldn't see. I let him go.

Discarding with shame my rolled newspaper,
I thought of him, back at the hive,
the Copernicus, the great Columbus of honey bees
with a wild tale of truth; misunderstood,
scoffed at by the loud drones.
A hero if I had killed him, perhaps;
instead I sent back a laughing stock.

I opened the window, let him
unawares outrun the loci of his graph.
He wobbled off on a third axis, dragging
his whine behind him, blundering
into what was no longer there, time
after time. He took the long way home:
he was already preparing his story.

August

In the long hayfields
a moon is wished for.

The nightjar purrs
remembering
what dawns have discovered; the ether
impales and cozens with stars.

The procession of poplars
is still. The exact words
are possible.

Not lovers
not poets are safe
amid the elegant luggage of nightfall.

Same Again

The trees enlarge the wind's vocabulary,
teaching it plurals.

Hourly, still, the train pulls
its shelf of lights this way, then that,
adding the sound later.

The stars on the kitchen window
are cometed by condensation.

Beyond that glass
the landscape turns another page
of a book I thought I knew;

it is heavier in the left hand than the right,
and I am a hopeful Orpheus
corking on a false moustache
to fetch Euridice a second time.

Methods of Winter

December waits
among the secret trees
for me to make the first move.

Streams creak, grass rings underhoof,
but snow hangs fire,
defining the silence.

The woods' gaunt legbones
lend each a shadow to darkness
making it whole.

Ice skims the cart-track;
makes two moons where one was
and I believe in both.

The Hard Harvest

The trees fell all one morning
and the next. I heard
cliffs crumble, the shingle of branches
shift and rip. Against silence
the tide of the woodland receded,
the chain-saw muttered technicalities.

Monosyllables – log, stake, chock –
now sum up what once
was a kindly dialect;
a whole course in rhetoric.

Gently this hard flesh falls
to circles, segments, arcs,
which, where they meet the air,
loose a surprising scent of lukewarm tea.

The tractor has stamped a double frown
on hessian floors where winter sky
shovels down, drab, tactless.
Shadows which leapt yesterday
are trapped now, under trunks,
in tight parallels. Smoke sways in loops.

The edge of the village is a strange
stride nearer. Beyond the lower woods,
beyond the railway, on the rising field
an old man stands on unborn primroses
and watches. In the garden his wife
stoops, whose last six months to live
began eight months ago.

Mirror in an Empty Room

Only an hour it took to jettison
this mirror's history. Ghosts,
the complementary colours of our losses,
prowl still at its edges,
but you must look away to see them.

You have to be thinking of something else
to hear the black kettle's chorus,
the soft tap
of embers falling softly
in a room as warm as a loaf.

The mirror hangs crooked;
it has been drinking for years
in its unofficial, oblong way.

It has given up obeying rules.
With its singular spaces, its green grins,
its lack of reliance on clocks,
this mirror has passed beyond theory.

It has absorbed the clatter of bottles
I slept through, the distant applause
of morning bacon in scoured pans,
the flap of cards, the tobacco glow
of paraffin-stove like clover on the ceiling,
the wink of glass, the clearing of throats
and the clearing of rooms.
It is busy now with the matter of mirrors.

A breeze blows from it as I climb
from past to present,
ruffles my hair indifferently
like an uncle at Christmas:
'So this is the young man.
Well, well, well. How he has grown .'

Rain on Hazel Leaves

Leaves deal with water audibly
    as eyes deal with shallows of spaces
which define themselves in terms of leaves,
    of watercoloured darkness, thickness
which is light still, but led another way
    and laid on air, shifting
to its muscles' flex. A slow
    counterpoint, an enharmonic change
of green to green through silver
    where the semiquavers of sweet rain,
a figured treble, bring down a scent
    of sky and gather weight
on surfaces. Quaver, crotchet, semibreve,
    then the raindrop breve lolls
to the sum of its rhythms, coils
    on edges, on rims of leaf bowed
against under-air, and grows
    to clear water-blossom, motionless
in the motion of the air. The meniscus burst
    is soundless: a simple vanishing,
un-petalling, and the sprung leaf leans
    in new improvisations; cadenzas
of damp woodland giving tongue
    to silence, the precious obverse
of these falling coins of light.